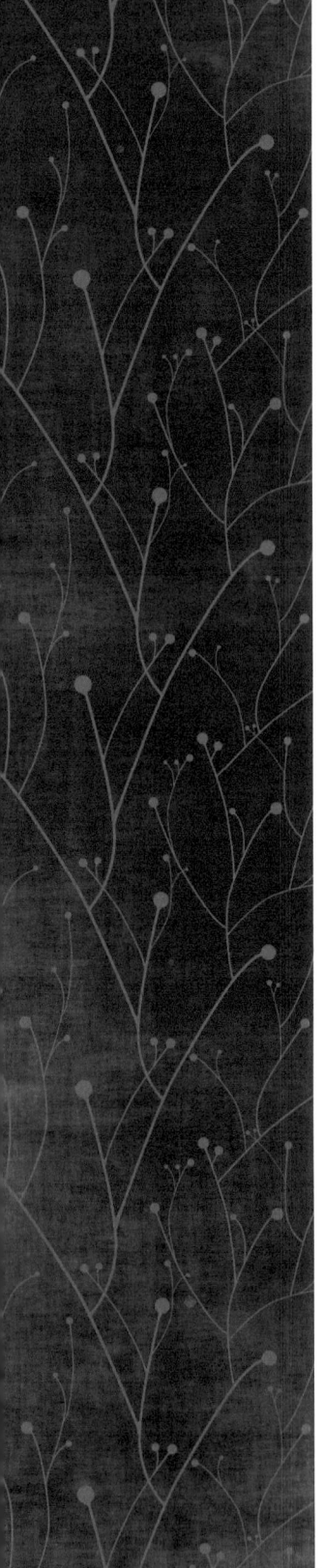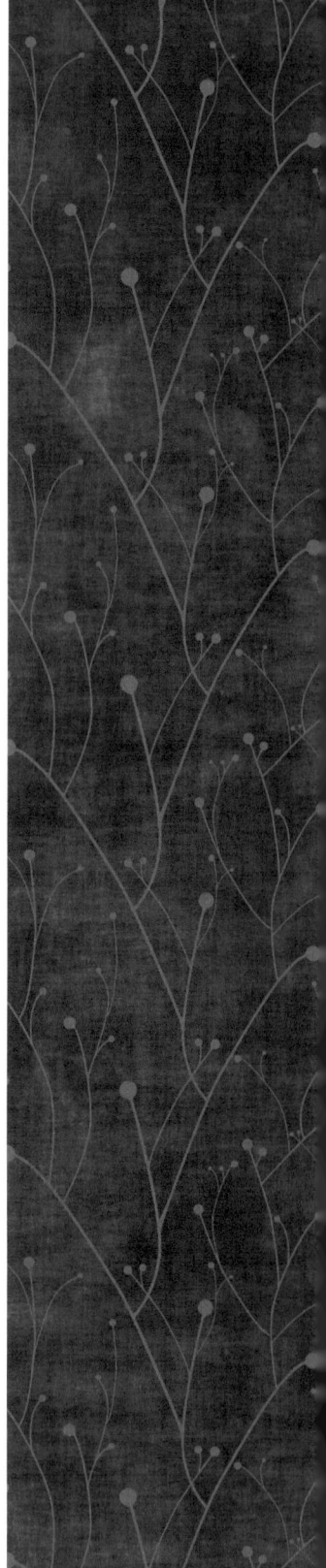

Table of Contents

X 2
Acknowledgement 3
Sharing of Mind 4

x Secrets & Seductions x

The Deal 8
We Feast! 9
Halves 10
I Blame You 11
Art of Tease 12
What About You? 13
The Aggressor 14
What's The Difference? 15
Oblivious 16
Age Old Exchange 17
Free to Be 18
Monotony 19
She Believes 20
Mockery 21
The Gift 23
Through Time 24
Poverty 25
For You 26
She is Gone 27
Sensual 28
Oh Innocence 29
Forbidden! 30
Cowardice 31
Kind Sir 32
One Who Leads 33
Mystery Within 34
In This Bed 35
Act of No Mercy 36
Secret 37

First published in the UK in 2010

First Edition October 2010

Publisher Sharon D Abel

ISBN 978-0-9567248-0-9
Nielson

Copyright 2010 Sharon D Abel

Sharon Abel has asserted her right under the copyright, designs and Patents Act. 1988 to be identified as the author of this work.

this book is sold subject to the conditions that it shall not, by way of trade or otherwise be lent, resold, hired out, or otherwise circulated in any form of binding or cover other than that in which it is published and without a similar condition, including this condition, being imposed on the subsequent purchaser.

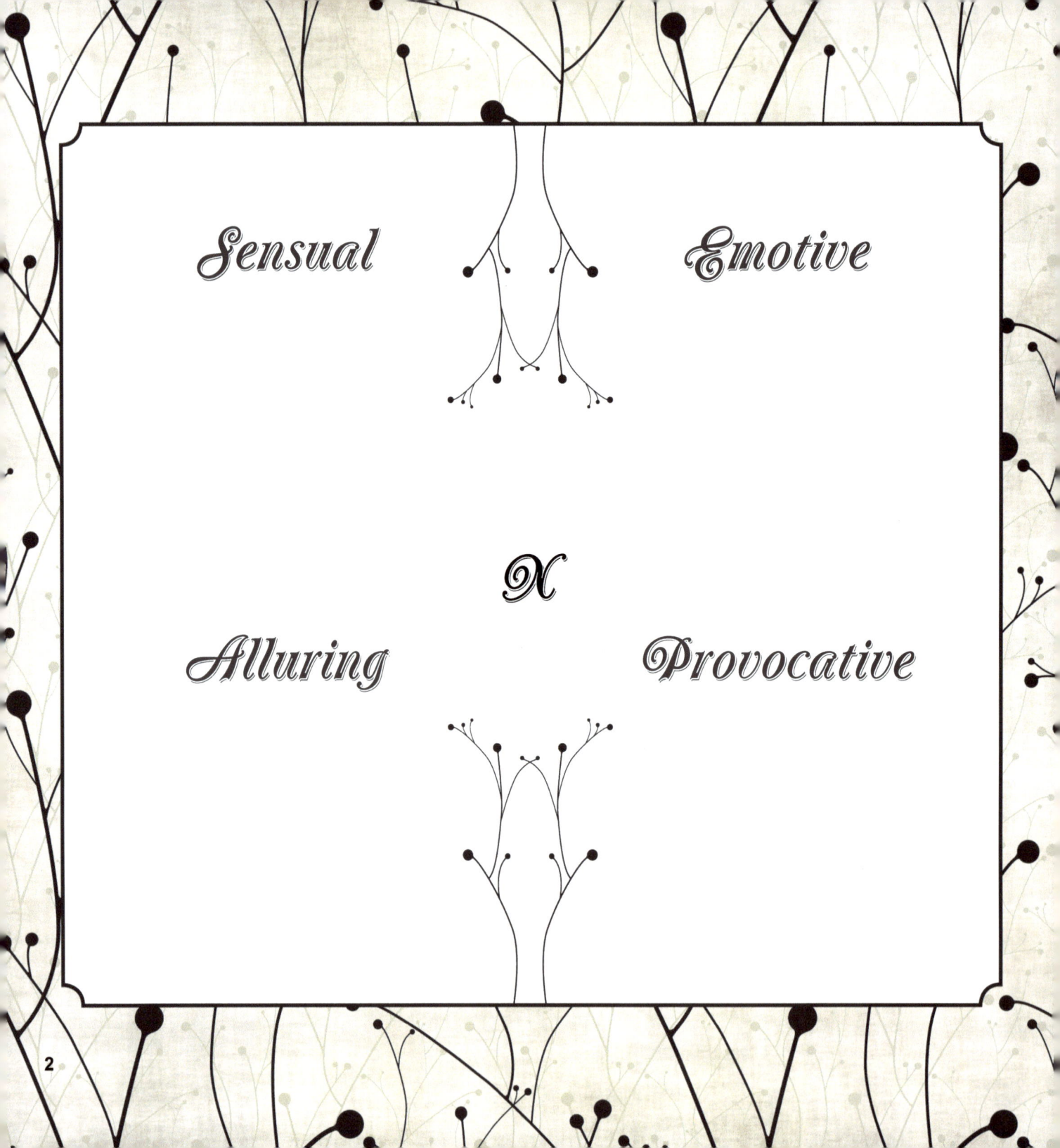

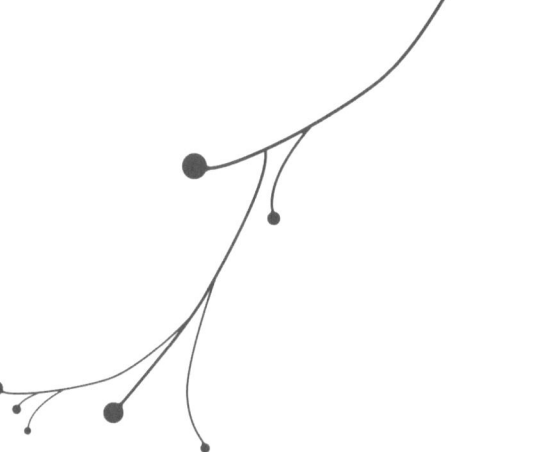

Acknowledgement

A huge thanks to Jon Tregenna, for his encouragement and feedback. I truly value his opinion and expertise as an accomplished writer.

To my lovely daughters,
Thanks for being 'you' x

Sharing of Mind

It flows.
The thoughts come tumbling out
Onto the page
Thoughts, once locked away

Memories, resurfaced
Times forgotten, reborn
Feelings, hidden within
Exposed, to enlighten
Reveal

Must show, educate
To change, adapt
More sides, more views
The burst of acknowledgement
Needed, to settle peacefully

To share, to burden
Not alone, united
In thoughts and imagery

Welcome to my world

x Secrets & Seductions x

The Deal

Perfect. Couldn't be more perfect
Spruced and wrapped
She to be envied, to be adored
She to be admired, to be craved

The look says it all
Tantalized, he visualised
What is to come, a done deal

Conversation freely flows
Between strangers
Where nothing is taboo
Undivided attention
By the hour

Nothing is too much
The food, the wine
The touch
The licking and slapping of lips
Anticipation, such anticipation

She to be cherished, fantasized
He to acquire the means to his desires
Flirty laughter, heads thrown back

She could find this no other way
Sharing in riches, delights
Sole focus, oh, the luxury
He is proud to showcase,
Display his feathers gold
For she is his, and his alone
For just one night…

Two souls who yearn acceptance
Two actors, playing out love
Would anyone suspect?
This charade?
No, for it is the most real
Love of the moment

He, grand gesture, pays their fill
A generous tip to waiting aides
A night of frivolity
To forget all else

Tonight is unreal. They are unreal
A planned performance, not yet ended
Even grander, he hands her the fee
For the theatrics been, and yet to be

The deal is sealed

We Feast!

Tonight, we eat my child
Tonight we feast!
Celebratory, in all its glory
All shades
all glowing

Fit for a king, fit for you
Chest puffed out
Self-satisfied
The requisite banquet
To display my kill

Go ahead
Gorge with wild abandon
Whilst I nimbly consume
Prided, aristocratic

No sacrifice to me
I provide, deft in my ability
Conquered, together
Feast my child, feast

Halves

Chipping away my outer self
The layers peeled back
Different sides of me

A woman of parts
Fragmented, divided
Composed as one
Glued by guise

Cleave the halves, look inside
Extreme polar of existence
Riches aplenty, rags galore
Divided by loyalties

Impressions stored
To be used, subdued
To advantage, to consequence

Mishandled baggage
Rousing conflict
Partial love, partial hate
Enveloped, blanketed
One package

I Blame You

Years of learning, achieving
Overcoming
Obstacles, huge obstacles
To gain my rightful place
To be trusted
In my role, abilities

Nearly there, the top
The top of my yearnings
To taste the fruit
Reap the rewards

Striving for what?
To have it all
And then….You
I blame you

Tearing me down
Where I am weakest
Yielding your power
Yielding your hatred

Do you know what you've done?
What you've destroyed?
Who has fallen in your wake?
Not just me
I blame you

That single act
Forcing me down
So you can look down
On me
Makes you feel taller
In the power you hold

What are you striving for?
What threatens you?
Must be me

What you yearn, you crush
Into compliance
What you fear, you trample
Into submission

The mere mention, mere sight
Revolts you
Threatens your armoured walls
Threatens what they see

Your superior existence
What have you achieved?
Those who bow around you
Your worshipping followers
You thrive
I wilt
In your shadow
I blame you

All by your side
Stand to attention
Or so you believe
Breeding contempt
You do this alone
I blame you

I blame me

Art of Tease

Blinkered in the spotlight
Awakened
By the hunger, the longing

The orectic figment
Coaxing fervour of passion

A coquette to male yearnings
Moving with grace, intent
Slowly, teasing apart
In wanton manner

Erotic display, to bait
To rouse the lascivious
Flaunting, tormenting
probing the frenzied mind

Shredding, layer upon layer
A quiet seduction
Flirting with greed
Tantalized curiosity

Dallying with desires
To control, ridicule
Toy with hope
Through whetted appetite

Divest of clothing
To reveal, to mock
Disrobed of mystery
The peak of lust
Reverberates

What About You?

"What about you?"
Yes! What about me!
"Don't Worry" I reply
My most sincere of tones
I'll do your 'duty' for you
Thinking begrudgingly
Should I just bolt?
All feelings of lust vanished

And yet, I'd so prepared
My wares displayed in grandure
Decorated to perfection
Your tastes, not mine

Serviced your every need
passion and accomplishment
The urge to please
The excitement to responses
of fulfilling every need
A need shared, at least by me

My needs secondary at that point
But why ask "What about you?"
Was my reply enough?
My needs, aren't needs shared it seems
You did not stir to satisfy

The Aggressor

Leather clad
She rules, inflicts
She to be obeyed
Faking fury
For benefit

Of no great height
Though tall, power yielding
Tall in respect
High in esteem

Whipping to submission

Freedom from her shackles
Of confinement
The upper hand
Binds the perverse

The aggressor!
The torturer!

Masked, concealing vulnerabilities
Of mercy
To abandon would expose
Fraudulence
A benevolent heroine
Sharing in the painful ache
For punishment
To desecrate

Who then more deserving
More receiving
Who then more giving

What's The Difference?

You, in your tweed suit of brown
Authoritive, knowledgeable
Knowledgeable in what?
Your own little box, your one side of life
So good, so righteous
Never a dark thought
Never the nerve to venture from your comfortable lie

He, in his shirt of silk
He has power over you
A freer existence, exploiting mans weakness
Bordering restrictions of law

Deemed immoral for his services
And yet, you seek his products for sale
You, hidden, sneaking to acquire
Him, open, enterprising, truthful

You envy him don't you?
The taboo, which he is able to live by, profit from
You are a slave to what he offers
A basic human need.

So, what's the difference?
You, the epitome of 'normality'
The educated, 'above board' business man
Him, the muted in society
The educated, keeper of men's fantasies

The difference, is your deceit
Your need for anonymity
Your need for 'normality'

Oblivious

Look at them, oblivious
If they knew
Knew the renegade
In their midst

Shatter their illusions
Of a seemingly pure society
A world away
Sat amongst them

Wanting to protest
'life is not that simple'
Judging others, deciding

A civilised meeting
Meeting of great minds?
Rather, acceptable minds
With influence

Reality, something else
Someone else
Not so
It is here

Feign understanding
Could not comprehend less
Rather turn a blind eye
Fellow being
Best at arms length

Just talk, all talk
Not charitable in heart
Words mean nothing
Fakery, they exude

The unthinkable
Sneaking in, viewing the charade
Their sheltered lives
Their upstanding aura
Reinforced by those less fortunate
Yet, unaware what breaths within
Within their sect
Oblivious

Age Old Exchange

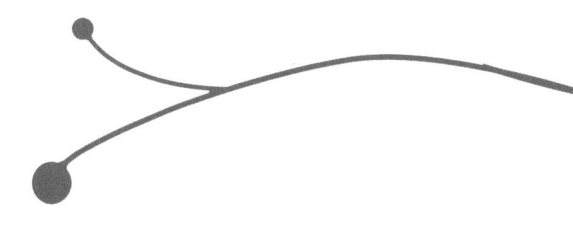

X

Shopping, browsing the aisles
Labels studied with intensity
Examining the merchandise
Stock of contraband

Gilded advert
Catching his eye
Amongst the bank of bullion
The one
Showcasing her wares
To be bartered in trade

Her mastery apparent
Displays her commodity
Of precious goods

What price for such purchase?
What worthy investment?
To share in profit

Sophisticated in craft
Marketed in shimmering gold

Currency both ways
An age old exchange

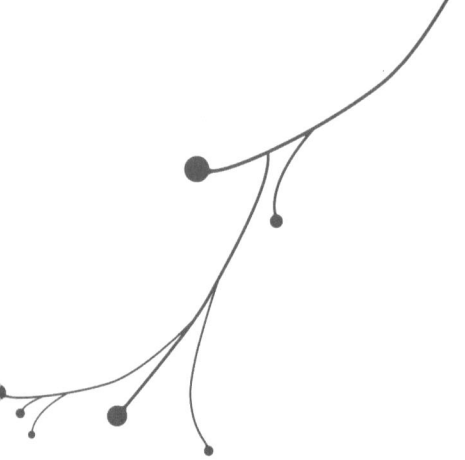

<u>Free to Be</u>

I've tasted freedom
Taken flight
Of fancy

I felt it
Hope, release from ego
Loved for me
The real entity

My true essence
Absorbed, breathed in
I took delight

Threw away the armour
The pretence
No consequence
Or care
For others perception

I was free
To shine
To be me

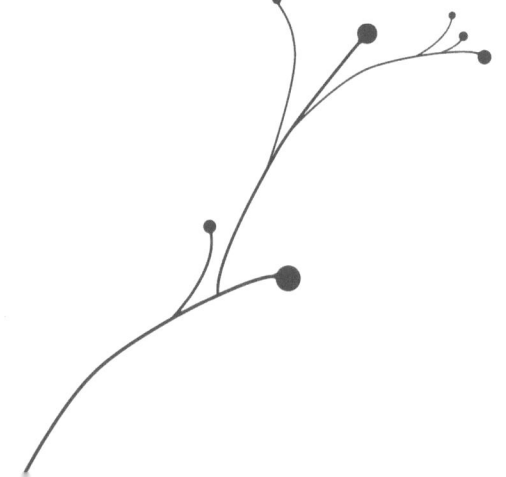

Monotony

Lifeless in monotone
Dulcet tones
The wearisome
Monotony

Day in, day out
Routine of task
Vanish in repetition
Seeking to diversion

Trudging through drudgery

All is colourless
It drones with humdrum patter
Subdued ambition
Ground into invisible mist

The mind-numbing
Pushed aside
By dreams to quell
Monotony

Emotions flat
Squashing hunger, drive
Too flaccid to rise to bait

The uniform binding
Held captive in tedium

Trapped in plain existence
Monotony

She Believes

Camouflage the eyes of depth
Gloss over cracks, of telling lines
Painted into semblance of youth
Of truth

The cloak which shrouds
The pretence
Concealing time
She believes
Smile, false as fact

Veiled in happiness
State of disguise, she perfects so well
Mixed with attire
To ward off inquisition

Costume complete, matching delusion
Colours bright, herself vibrant
She believes

Let pantomime begin
To obscure the reality
Masked into acceptance
And welcomed with open arms
Not alone in fakery

They are fooled, it seems
She believes

A sham, to protect
Curved lips, not meeting eye
The farce is well received
Well practiced

The illusion undiscovered
She believes

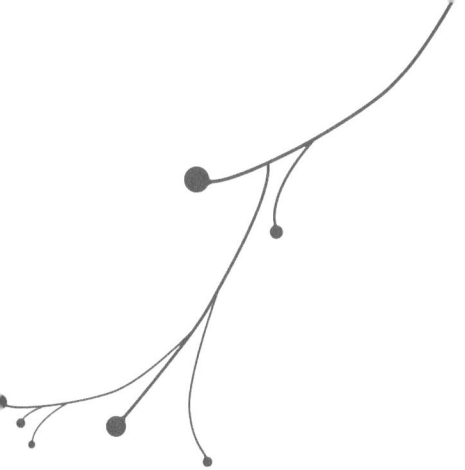

Mockery

For my own good
You're right, I know
Overstepping the mark
Of familiarity
Of insolence

You must really care
Such attention to detail
Noting my idiocies
My failures

Thank you for educating
For protecting
Making me all yours

Pushed the wrong buttons
Didn't I?
Over the edge, with frustration
Not your fault

Taking the time
To tend my wounds
Like no one else would
So well hidden now

Your devotion endears me
Constantly vigilant
To my every move

Today
Today, I was stupid
Turned a mans head
Can't calm the inevitable
Time to repent
I expect

The Gift

Music softly drifts
Drifting, wafting, enticing
Hips slowly swaying
Eyes closed, consuming the energy
The energy of joy
Excitement, pure exhilaration

Holding the dress close
She sways, her invisible partner
Turning, dancing, displaying

Fine silk no less
Caressing and soothing
Placed lovingly on the bed
With a wink of anticipation

The lotion applied
Smell of decadence
Rich, fulfilling
The scent of romance, longing
Hands sliding upwards
Gently stroking, moistened
The scent of a woman
To entice, she smiles

The matching lace
Delicate within hand
Powerful with effect
Placed to adorn the prize

Sheer stockings of black
Slowly, teasingly stretched
Upon each slender thigh
Clipped in place
Though not for purpose

The silk now draped
Perfect colour
Red. She mused
Enough to rouse the most mundane

Hair, folded into bouncing curls
To rest on shoulders glistening
To drape on mounds
Heaving, with breaths of desire

Face adorned with hues of innocence
Yet subtle savagery
Lips of blushing pink
Resembling the hidden gift

A flair of sophistication
The string of pearls
Rolled gently between finger and thumb
Attached with rolling beat of drum
Spritz of perfume
Set to dazzle, lure

Slipping into shoes bejewelled
The finale, she smirks
Pressing down the cloth
That skims her, wraps her

She is ready, ritual complete
Expert, accomplished
Her work half way done

A present, though not free
To be unwrapped
In haste, in greed
She smiles, and leaves

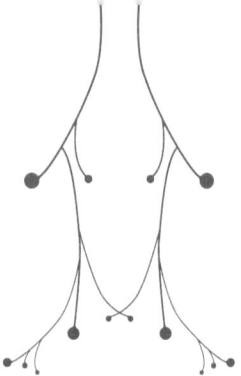

Through Time

To leave our mark
Upon this world
Words through time
Still relevant in meaning

Pulsing through veins
Mapped in flesh
Centuries of instinct
Wisdom

Stories of flair
Re-enacted, despaired
Time and time again
Failing
Overcoming adversity

Trials of longing
Repeat liaisons
The past unbeknown
To those ignorant in bliss

Same lessons, same tales
In emotive form
Inspiring answers craved
Belonging, camaraderie

Words through time

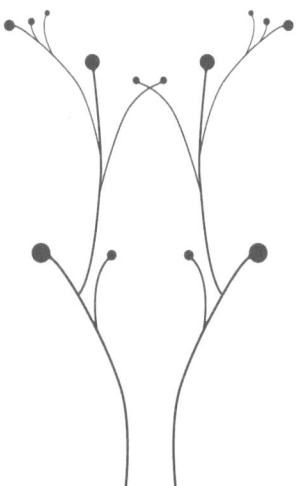

Poverty

Sometimes, by circumstance
do our choices reduce?
Perhaps taken away
Necessity, a priority

Human need
Basic human need
Poverty of love, finance, means
creates a rebellion within us
to protect others, ourselves

How can we provide
without these three
Relied upon, unquestioning
and do what must be done

Do or die!
Demise or survive
What takes over logic?
Or maybe it's logic which prevails

Demeaned, in order to nurture
As low, as low as can go
Not seemingly acceptable
In society's eyes

Who judges? And why?
Perhaps unknowing beings
who have no needs withdrawn
Frivolous, in their riches
Frivolous, in their ignorance

For You

A little bit of me, I give to you
Use it wisely
Treat it kind
For it is delicate, breakable
A mosaic of rainbow glass

Warm to the touch
Breathing life into your core

Be gentle, and nurture it
It will grow
Grow around you, encompass you
It can protect, with folded wings

Don't harm it
For it is fragile
Fragile as tissue paper
Pink, and fluttering around you

Careful where you tread
Don't crush
Contains crystals of pure beauty
Sparkling with vigour
Offers zest for life

Keep it
Go on, keep it
I want you to have it
In safe hands, I'm sure

Look after it for me

I can trust you
Can't I ?

She is Gone

She is pitiful, my friend
A sight to behold
And yet to revere
Childlike, youthful in outlook
Yet, withered and torn

A graceful beauty
Without the grace
A figment of a mans imagination
Though real, though available

Delicate upon appearance
Peering from beneath her shell
Hardened, so hardened
To what comes her way

Once famed for her elegance
Now famed for her deeds
She uses, is used
Plays the game to perfection

She is gone, my friend
Into the black abyss
Of cruelty, slavery
Reliance on what she detests

Swallowed up by advantage
They all take advantage
Pierce her weakness
Thrust into obscurity

Taken to the underworld
To ride the spoils of life
Coming up for air
She gasps infrequently

Damaged, lost
Though sought, and found
Dragged back down

Sensual

Conceal your eyes
Discharged of sight
So that you may feel
Light of touch
With feather
Silk

Devoid of sound
Hot breath upon your skin
Travelling down
Your spine of consciousness

Withdraw in silence
Curb your tongue
Smothered in sensation

Bind your hands
To feel released
To me
Unleashed

Use your mind
Keep your nerve
Pulsating
Tingling

Feel the tactile
Anticipation
Liberation

Air charged
Orbs of stimulation
Hair, brushing strokes
Hint of contact
Skin to skin

Taste the ambience
Flavour the submission
Subdued, lulled
Fulfilled

Soaking up the pleasure
Throb of longing

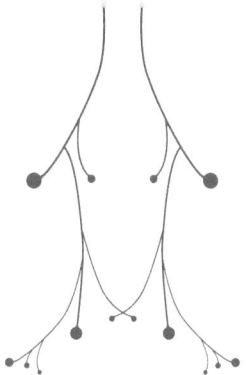

Oh Innocence

Oh innocence
I worry for you
You've no idea
Of lurking danger
Threatening
Your trusting soul

Innocence
I can advise
But you must learn
Train your expectations
As you will know

Innocence
They will take from you
That which makes you

Self satisfied to conquer
You
like a beacon
Of challenge

Innocence
You'll be changed
Suspicion of intent
Alert to those
Who wish you harm

Oh innocence
In time
You will use your guile
To destroy
That which is innocent

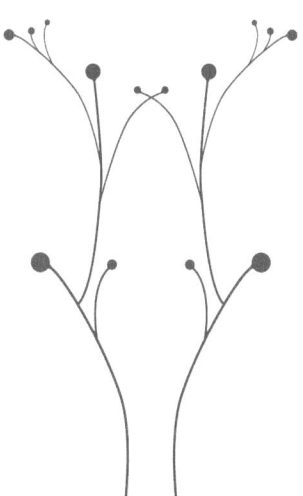

Forbidden!

I don't want to hear it!
Entertain it
Believe it
I forbid it
It's forbidden

I already know it

Won't share your guilt
Out of bounds
Beyond your reach
Beyond your taking

Don't say it
Don't think it
Nor recall it
I forbid it!

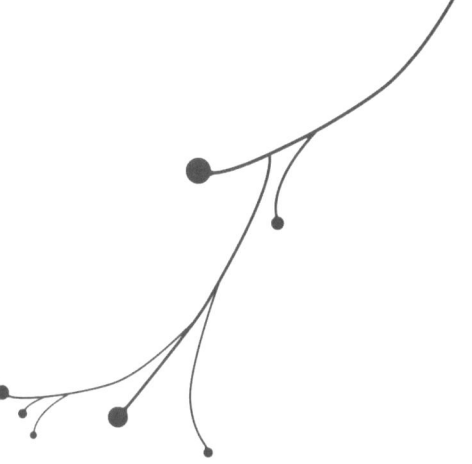

Cowardice

What are you afraid of?
Despicable coward
Me? Them? Everything?
Quaking in your boots

Exaggerating your strength
The gallant one
Galloping to the rescue
You'd have them believe

Hiding your timidity
Shrinking away from challenge
Out of sight

Turning tail
Fear of exposing your panic
Your lack of fortitude
Lack of backbone

The shaking hero
nerves of no steel
Hesitate to show your 'courage'

No nerve to speak of
No brave heart
Cowardice

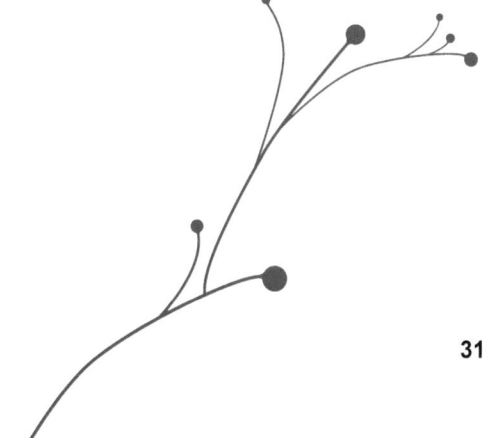

Kind Sir

'What would you like to hear?
Kind Sir
How your eyes
Capture my sole?'
Feel them moving, studying
Every curve, every inch

'Your words move me
Kind Sir
Imagining your lips on mine
The ecstasy held within
Your expert words
Your expert tongue…..'

'I am breathless
Kind Sir
Your slight of hand
Brushing, teasingly
Along my arm'
Circle open palm
Weaving fingers

'I am not easy
Kind Sir'
Your smile, intended reassurance
Though arrogance emits
So sure, so determined
We know
A coy response
Illusions of power, conquest
Part of the game

'I am won over
Kind Sir
Nothing yearned more
As now'

'How do you do it?
Kind Sir
Bring me to my weakened knees
You the prize catch
How lucky am I?'
How lucky indeed

One Who Leads

Claws of razor sharp
Grabbing, clutching
Gnarling teeth
Nipping, gnawing
All in play

Mischief sparkling, challenging
Eyes wide
Black, penetrating
Goading

Evocative of youth
Of foolery
Darting forward, gripped
Fierce in fight

Trusting, inquisitive
Urging more, more play
Rolling to the softer side
Exposed, to lure

Promise of privilege
Permission to fuss, stroke
The ego, the finesse

Has trained you well
Her minion of desires
Subordinate of deserving
Love, and be loved

Leading the way
Rules to abide
The rewards are worthy
If compliant
Mishandle at your peril
For she will be gone

Mystery Within

Upon meeting
Were you intrigued?
Intrigued by me?
Anxious to enquire
Of my mystery within

Too soon perhaps
Time needed to acquaint
Mustn't be impolite
Probing, delving
you may think

But four months past
Your patience weary
As I query your notions
Your previous existence
My keen, eager chatter
Unsettles you

You don't share
Any part of you
So unaware of me
Your apathy
Unnerving

Dispassionate of my revelations
Of no concern to you
The future, you say?
I have not known you, before that day
The day we met

Self-absorbed, in the here and now
Detached from what bought you here
Us here
You have no history
Nor I, it seems
Nothing to relate
What's to communicate?

So aloof, shrug it off
Frustrated at your numbness
No memories to laugh about?
Experience to share?

Be alert, let me reflect
No, your pomposity reverberates
Impassive, indifferent
From me
No interest
Of my mystery within

Were you ever here
Before that day?

In This Bed

We are not alone
You and I
In this bed

They surround us
The origins of all
In which we partake

Familiar history, now prevalent
In what we do
A mind full of lovers
From which we connect

You osculate
With those that existed
Before you

Reminisce, at time of private encounter
Bring the past into now
To enhance

Journey of discovery
Coached me here
Cherished liaisons
Regrets

We are not alone
You and I
In this bed

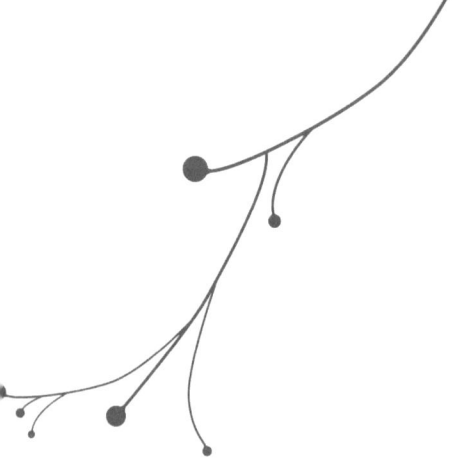

Act of No Mercy

Act one
They meet on snowy hill
Designed romance
In glare of frosted mounds
He takes her hand
In gentle clasp
Woos in lilt of poetry

Act two
He phones five times a day
In eager tone
To bait, to snare
Keep her interest high
Floating, swirling
Giddy with longing
Sees the man, that she could marry

Act three
He leads her up the stair of promise
Both in triumph
In haste, to seal
Unite them both
They writhe
Beneath the satin sheets
Of ecstasy

Act four
No more

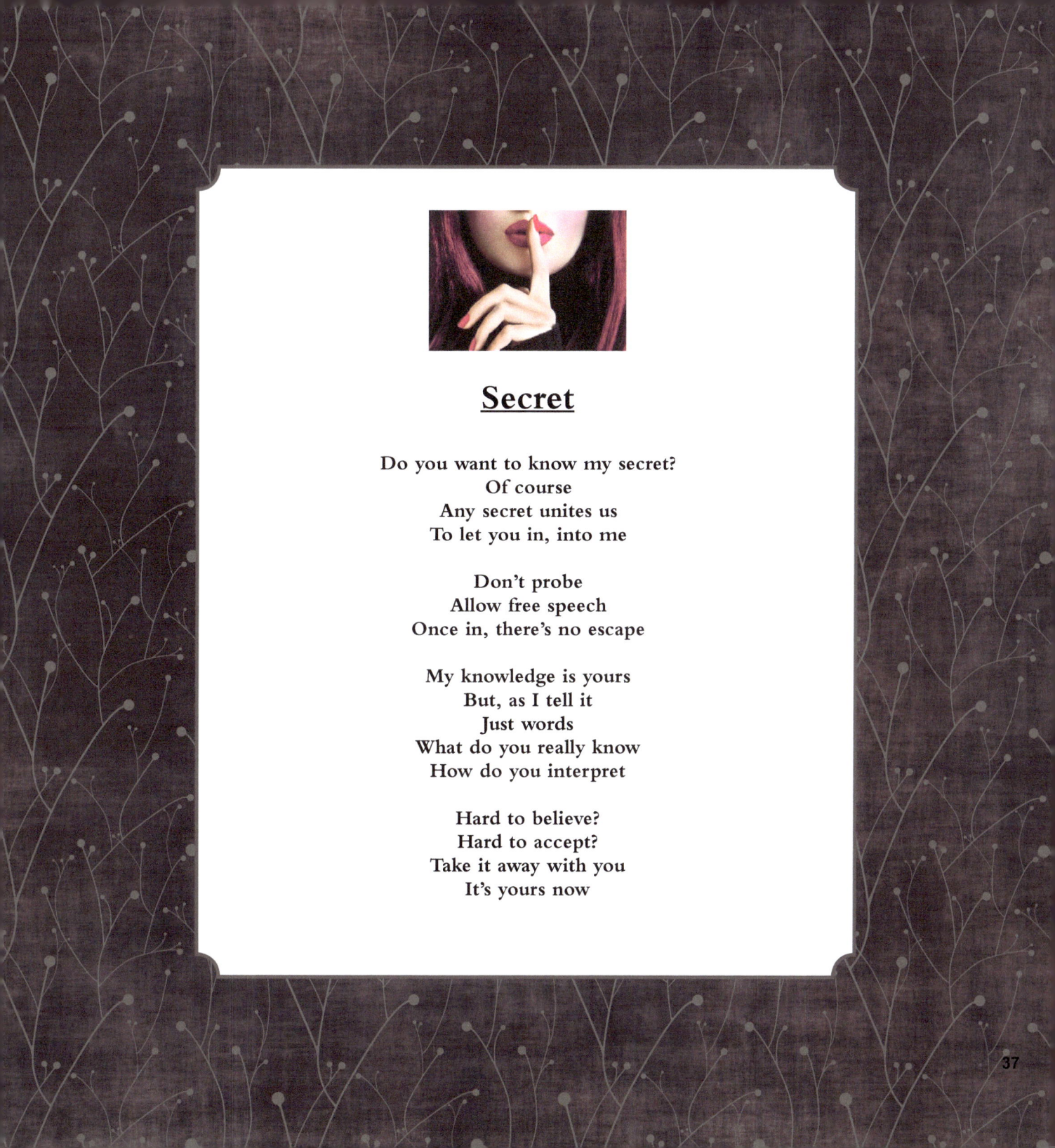

<u>Secret</u>

Do you want to know my secret?
Of course
Any secret unites us
To let you in, into me

Don't probe
Allow free speech
Once in, there's no escape

My knowledge is yours
But, as I tell it
Just words
What do you really know
How do you interpret

Hard to believe?
Hard to accept?
Take it away with you
It's yours now

www.ingramcontent.com/pod-product-compliance
Lightning Source LLC
Chambersburg PA
CBHW040057160426
43192CB00002B/95